Listen
Sh'ma

By Rabbi Alyson Solomon

Illustrated by Bryony Clarkson

APPLES & HONEY PRESS

Dedicated to and inspired by my daughter,
Sybil Leeba, whose love oozes joy. Blessed by you.
—RAS

For Finn, Scarlett, and Madeleine
— BC

**Sh'ma means "listen" in Hebrew.
Listen Sh'ma is inspired by a Jewish prayer about
oneness and love, when we sleep and when we wake.**

The illustrations for this book were created using a combination of
cut-paper collage, acrylic and watercolor paint, and colored pencil.
The original artwork was scanned and lightly enhanced with digital
processing to complete the illustrations.

Apples & Honey Press
An Imprint of Behrman House Publishers
Millburn, New Jersey 07041
www.applesandhoneypress.com

ISBN 978-1-68115-611-8

Library of Congress Catalog Number: 2022056161

Design by Leslie Mechanic
Art direction by Ann D. Koffsky
Edited by Dena Neusner
Printed in China

1 3 5 7 9 8 6 4 2

Sh'ma means "listen."
Shhh-mmm-ahhh

Shhh is the sound of splashing warm water in the bubbly tub.

Shhh is the sound of
zipping beautiful bodies
into fresh jammies.

Shhh is the sound of whispering sweet stories in the quiet house.

Shhh...

Shhh-mmm-ahhh

Mmmm is the sound of

drinking warm milk

in the old rocking chair.

Mmmm is the sound of letting out belly breaths in the changing light.

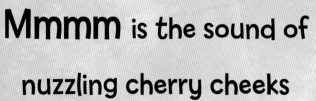

Mmmm is the sound of nuzzling cherry cheeks hugged in close.

Mmmm

Shhh–mmm–ahhh

Ahhh is the sound of

smiling joyfully,

in bed at last.

Ahhh is the sound of stretching long legs under cozy covers.

Ahhh is the sound of singing songs of love and prayers for peace.

Ahhh

Shhh

Mmm

Ahhh

Shhh

Mmm

Ahhh

Shhh-mmm-ahhh
Sh'ma.
Listen to the world.
Listen to love.
Listen.

Dear Families,

Sh'ma means "listen" in Hebrew. When we say the six words of the Sh'ma prayer, we declare the Oneness of God. We say a giant, heartfelt "YES!" to love and tender caring. When we take care of ourselves and those we love, we magnify God's love in the world.

When we lay down and when we rise up, the Sh'ma invites us to pause and notice our body, our family, and the blessings of our day. We say the Sh'ma when our hearts are full, as well as when we're scared, and when we don't know what else to say. The Sh'ma is there for whatever we need, whenever we need it. Our Sh'ma changes and grows as we change and grow.

By slowing down the first word of the Sh'ma prayer—shhh, mmm, ahhh—we slow down to hear the sounds of the world around us and within us. Listen close. What are the sounds of love that you hear in the world?

Wishing you closeness,

Rabbi Alyson Solomon

Sh'ma Yisrael
Listen, Israel

Adonai Eloheinu
Our God

Adonai Echad
Is One